Betty Aspinall

LENT WITH ST MARK

Forty Days of Prayer

Richard Garrard

LENT WITH ST MARK

Forty Days of Prayer

Richard Garrard

Kevin Mayhew

First published in 1992 by
KEVIN MAYHEW LTD
Rattlesden
Bury St Edmunds
Suffolk IP30 0SZ

© 1992 Kevin Mayhew Ltd

The publishers wish to thank the following for permission to
reproduce copyright material:

The British and Foreign Bible Society for all passages from
St Mark's Gospel, Today's English Version.

The Liturgical Psalter for all ASB psalm passages

*The Division of Christian Education of the National Council of
the Church of Christ in the USA* for passages from Isaiah,
Philippians and Colossians, Revised Standard Version,
© 1946, 1952 and 1971.

All other acknowledgements are to be found on or near
the page to which they refer.

ISBN   0 86209 297 3

Front cover: *A Male Saint* (detail), identified as St. Mark,
by Giovanni Battista Cima da Conegliano (c. 1459-1517).
Reproduced by courtesy of the Trustees,
The National Gallery, London.

Cover design by Juliette Clarke
Typesetting and Page Creation by Anne Haskell
Printed and bound in Great Britain.

CONTENTS

Two warnings go with this book:

1 Do not strain to be super-holy. Let the words and images flow over you. You can always come back to a section at some later time, and you are likely to find that the second time round will yield new thoughts, pictures and prayers quite different from those which came to you previously. This is all to the good. Creativity is often a matter of rearranging familiar thoughts to discover whole new worlds of meaning and devotion.

2 Prayer is adventure. It does change you. It does enlarge your mind and throw new shafts of light onto set ideas and conventional assumptions. Do expect God to change you, and then he will!

The Bible translation of St Mark's Gospel through this book is Today's English version, which offers a simple uncluttered style and puts some passages in refreshingly clear ways.

INTRODUCTION

LENT HAS FORTY DAYS

- The time Jesus spent in the desert to prepare for his public ministry;

- One day for each year the Jewish people travelled the desert, seeking their Promised Land;

- And in the early Church, new Christians used Lent to receive instruction in their faith and prepare for their Baptism at Easter.

Today Christians still keep the forty days as a special time for praying, thinking and reflecting, seeking to know God more deeply and to grow in love for him.

This is not a book about prayer but a series of orders of prayer which you are invited to use as laid out or adapt as you find most helpful.

The simple aim of this collection of readings and prayers is to encourage you to set aside time to do these things, and help you to pray with imagination and interest throughout Lent: to follow the way of Jesus more closely and to celebrate his victory of sin and death in his Easter Triumph.

The method is to put Bible readings beside non-biblical material to stimulate thought and prayer, offering new insights, new angles of vision, new ways of focusing on God. The readings offer a basis for prayer in one's own words, pointers for further investigation, starting-points for discussion.

Each order of service has within the formula:

PICTURE • PONDER • PRAY • PROMISE

These words are an invitation to let your mind run on the readings so that ideas, vision, prayers and resolutions can result. Be adventurous, think wide, but always seek to return in thought and prayer to the God who is alive and whose love for us never fails. Bring him thanks, sorrow and requests; let your imagination be set on fire.

Each order is designed to be used by two or more people but you can use them just as well on your own, in a quiet place, or a railway train, in the morning or evening, or whenever you can find time to pray.

If used by a group, the picture • ponder • pray • promise section can be a time for shared prayer and discussion. But equally it can be a time of silence for each person to use as they wish. You will notice that the Response sections have been printed in bold and medium type to encourage one person to lead and others to respond.

If used alone, then a note-book or any scrap of paper can help the praying process by brief notes, jottings or pictures to engage and use all our faculties in focusing on God – Creator, Saviour, Spirit.

O Lord, open our lips:
And our mouth shall proclaim your praise.
O Lord, open our minds:
And the mind of Christ shall be in us.
O Lord, open our hearts:
And your truth will flow to others.

READING: PSALM 90:1-6 AND 12

O Lord, you have been our refuge:
    from one generation to another.

Before the mountains were born
or the earth and the world were brought to be:
    from eternity to eternity you are God.

You turn man back into dust:
    saying, 'Return to dust you sons of Adam'.

For a thousand year in your sight
are like yesterday passing:
    or like one watch of the night.

You cut them short like a dream:
    like the fresh grass of the morning;

in the morning it is green and flourishes:
    at evening it is withered and dried up.

Teach us so to number our days:
    that we may apply our hearts to wisdom.

READING: MARK 1:1-13

John the Baptist and the Baptism
and Temptation of Jesus

This is the Good News about Jesus Christ, the Son of God.
It began as the prophet Isaiah had written:
    'God said, "I will send my messenger ahead of you
    to clear the way for you."
Someone is shouting in the desert,
    "Get the road ready for the Lord;
    make a straight path for him to travel!"'

So John appeared in the desert, baptising and preaching. 'Turn away from your sins and be baptised,' he told the people, 'and God will forgive your sins.' Many people from the province of Judaea and the city of Jerusalem went out to hear John. They confessed their sins, and he baptised them in the River Jordan.

John wore clothes made of camel's hair, with a leather belt round his waist, and his food was locusts and wild honey. He announced to the people, 'The man who will come after me is much greater than I am. I am not good enough even to bend down and untie his sandals. I baptise you with water, but he will baptise you with the Holy Spirit.'

Not long afterwards Jesus came from Nazareth in the province of Galilee, and was baptised by John in the Jordan. As soon as Jesus came up out of the water, he saw heaven opening and the Spirit coming down on him like a dove. And a voice came from heaven, 'You are my own dear Son. I am pleased with you.'

At once the Spirit made him go into the desert, where he stayed forty days, being tempted by Satan. Wild animals were there also, but angels came and helped him.

PICTURE • PONDER • PRAY • PROMISE

A PRAYER

Lord Jesus, dear Son of God,
We thank you for Lent;
Help us to know your love
And to be sorry for our sins;
Burn out our pride;
Fill us with gratitude and peace
This day and every day. Amen.

Pray for people in despair and times of sorrow,
Pray for those tempted into evil and sin,
Pray for yourself and for strength to live
   in the Way of Jesus.

O give thanks to the Lord for he is good:
His mercy endures for ever.
I will walk with the Lord:
In the land of the living.

O Lord, open our lips:
And our mouth shall proclaim your praise.
Call us to your service:
And make us worthy of the calling.

READING: MARK 1:14-20

Jesus Calls Four Fisherman

After John the Baptist had been put in prison, Jesus went to Galilee and preached the Good News from God. 'The right time has come,' he said, 'and the Kingdom of God is near! Turn away from your sins and believe the Good News!'

As Jesus walked along the shore of Lake Galilee, he saw two fishermen, Simon and his brother Andrew, catching fish with a net. Jesus said to them 'Come with me, and I will teach you to catch men.' At once they left their nets and went with him.

He went a little farther on and saw two other brothers, James and John, the sons of Zebedee. They were in their boat getting their nets ready. As soon as Jesus saw them, he called them; they left their father Zebedee in the boat with the hired men and went with Jesus.

READING: PSALM 32:9-11

I will instruct you
and direct you in the way that you should go:
    I will fasten my eye upon you
      and give you counsel.
Be not like horse or mule that have no understanding:
    whose forward course must be curbed with bit
      and bridle.
Great tribulations remain for the ungodly:
    but whoever puts his trust in the Lord
      mercy embraces him on every side.

PICTURE • PONDER • PRAY • PROMISE

A Prayer

> Father, Son, Holy Spirit,
> We thank you for the earliest disciples.
> Help us to follow your way
> In all we think, or say, or do. Amen.

Thank God for the truth and the love of
  the Gospel of Jesus;
Thank God for the faith of all who have followed
  the Christian way through the centuries;
Pray for those who have no faith;
Pray for those who are lost in the confusions
  of the world, especially those without family or friends;
Pray for yourself and for grace to follow Jesus.

> Lord, to whom shall we turn?
> **You alone have the words of eternal life.**
> Call us to your service:
> **And make us worthy of the calling.**

O Lord, open our lips:
And our mouth shall proclaim your praise
Praise God with all your heart:
Let us praise his holy name.

READING: MARK 1:21-28

A Man With an Evil Spirit

Jesus and his disciples came to the town of
Capernaum, and on the next Sabbath Jesus went to the
synagogue and began to teach. The people who heard
him were amazed at the way he taught, for he wasn't like
the teachers of the Law; instead, he taught with authority.

Just then a man with an evil spirit in him came into
the synagogue and screamed, 'What do you want with
us, Jesus of Nazareth? Are you here to destroy us? I know
who you are – you are God's holy messenger!'

Jesus ordered the spirit, 'Be quiet, and come out of
the man!'

The evil spirit shook the man hard, gave a loud
scream, and came out of him. The people were all so
amazed that they started saying to one another, 'What is
this? Is it some kind of new teaching? This man has
authority to give orders to the evil spirits, and they obey
him!'

And so the news about Jesus spread quickly everywhere in the province of Galilee.

READING: PSALM 103:6-13

The Lord works righteousness:
    And justice for all who are oppressed.
He made known his ways to Moses:
    And his works to the children of Israel.
The Lord is full of compassion and mercy:
    Slow to anger and of great goodness.

He will not always be chiding:
   Nor will he keep his anger for ever.
He has not dealt with us according to our sins:
   Nor rewarded us according to our wickedness.
For as the heavens are high above the earth:
   So great is his mercy over those that fear him.

PICTURE • PONDER • PRAY • PROMISE

A PRAYER

   Jesus, Lord of all the world,
   We praise your healing power,
   Heal us from all evil in our lives
   To love and follow you each day. Amen.

Thank God for his healing power:
   for doctors, surgeons and nurses,
   for all who work for those sick in body, mind and spirit,
   for your own doctor;

Pray that the Church may play its full part in the healing
work of Jesus.

   Lord, to whom shall we go?
   Your healing Gospel is eternal life.
   Lord use us in your healing work:
   And let us bring life and hope to others.

O Lord, open our lips:
And our mouth shall proclaim your praise.
Your love and your truth last for ever:
We long to follow your laws.

READING: LINES FROM 'THE ROCK' BY T.S. ELIOT

The world turns and the world changes,
But one thing does not change.
In all my years, one thing does not change.
However you disguise it, this thing does not change:
The perpetual struggle of Good and Evil.
Forgetful, you neglect your shrines and churches;
The men you are in these times deride
What has been done of good, you find explanations
To satisfy the rational enlightened mind.
Second, you neglect and belittle the desert.
The desert is not remote in southern tropics,
The desert is not only around the corner,
The desert is squeezed in the tube-train next to you,
The desert is in the heart of your brother.

READING: MARK 1 32-39

Jesus: Preaching and Healing

After the sun had set and evening had come, people
brought to Jesus all the sick and those who had demons.
All the people of the town gathered in front of the house.
Jesus healed many who were sick with all kinds of
diseases and drove out many demons. He would not let
the demons say anything, because they knew who he
was.

Very early the next morning, long before daylight,
Jesus got up and left the house. He went out of the town
to a lonely place, where he prayed. But Simon and his
companions went out searching for him, and when they
found him, they said, 'Everyone is looking for you.'

But Jesus answered, 'We must go on to the other villages round here. I have to preach in them also, because that is why I came.'

So he travelled all over Galilee, preaching in the synagogues and driving out demons.

PICTURE · PONDER · PRAY · PROMISE

A Prayer

Lord, wherever I go, whatever I do,
Be alive in my heart,
That in the crowdedness of life,
I may know the peace of faith in you,
My healer and my friend. Amen.

Pray for people who are lonely, friendless and afraid;
Thank God for the true peace and silence that faith
offers to us all,
And pray to know how to share your faith with others.

Lord, to whom shall we go?
You have the word of eternal life and peace.

The lines by T. S. Eliot are from Chorus 1 of 'The Rock', *Collected Poems 1090-1962*, and are reproduced by permission of the publisher, Faber and Faber Ltd.

O Lord, open our lips:
And our mouth shall proclaim your praise.
In your mercy I live:
For your law is my delight.

READING: MARK 2:1-12

Jesus Heals a Man Paralysed in Body and in Spirit

Jesus went back to Capernaum, and the news spread that he was at home. So many people came together that there was no room left, not even out in front of the door. Jesus was preaching the message to them when four men arrived, carrying a paralysed man to Jesus. Because of the crowd, however, they could not get the man to him. So they made a hole in the roof right above the place where Jesus was. When they had made an opening, they let the man down, lying on his mat. Seeing how much faith they had, Jesus said to the paralysed man, 'My son, your sins are forgiven.'

Some teachers of the Law who were sitting there thought to themselves, 'How does he dare talk like this? This is blasphemy! God is the only one who can forgive sins!'

At once Jesus knew what they were thinking, so he said to them, 'Why do you think such things? Is it easier to say to this paralysed man, "Your sins are forgiven", or to say, "Get up, pick up your mat, and walk"? I will prove to you, then, that the Son of Man has authority on earth to forgive sins.' So he said to the paralysed man, 'I tell you, get up, pick up your mat, and go home!'

While they all watched, the man got up, picked up his mat, and hurried away. They were all completely amazed and praised God, saying, 'We have never seen anything like this!'

Christ for the world we sing!
The world to Christ we bring with fervent prayer;
The wayward and the lost
By restless passions tossed,
Redeemed at countless cost from dark despair.

Christ for the world we sing!
The world to Christ we bring with one accord;
With us the work to share,
With us reproach to dare,
With us the cross to bear for Christ our Lord.

Christ for the world we sing!
The world to Christ we bring with joyful song;
The new-born souls, whose days,
Reclaimed for error's ways,
Inspired with hope and praise, to Christ belong.

PICTURE • PONDER • PRAY • PROMISE

A PRAYER

Lord, as his friends brought a man to you for healing,
May we, by prayer, word and example,
Bring others to know you for themselves. Amen.

Thank God for his healing power
    for the Church's ministry of healing,
    and for a growing of that ministry at the present time.

Pray for all who care for the sick, the poor, the oppressed
    for all who have no-one who cares for them,
    for all who need the release of forgiveness.

Praise God for Christ who sets us free in body,
    mind and spirit!

Lord, to whom shall we go?
You have the words of eternal life.
Lord, make us whole in body, mind and spirit.
And bring others to you for healing.

O give thanks to the Lord for he is good:
His mercy endures for ever.
Whoever loves is a child of God:
For God is love.

READING: MARK 2:13-17

Jesus and the Outcasts of Society

Jesus went back again to the shore of Lake Galilee. A crowd came to him, and he started teaching them. As he walked along, he saw a tax collector, Levi son of Alphaeus, sitting in his office. Jesus said to him, 'Follow me.' Levi got up and followed him.

Later on Jesus was having a meal in Levi's house. A large number of tax collectors and other outcasts were following Jesus, and many of them joined him and his disciples at the table. Some teachers of the Law, who were Pharisees, saw that Jesus was eating with these outcasts and tax collectors, so they asked his disciples, 'Why does he eat with such people?'

Jesus heard them and answered 'People who are well do not need a doctor, but only those who are sick. I have not come to call respectable people, but outcasts.'

READING: 'LOVE BADE ME WELCOME' BY GEORGE HERBERT

Love bade me welcome, yet my soul drew back,
Guilty of dust and sin.
But quick-eyed love, observing me grow slack
From my first entrance in,
Drew nearer to me, sweetly questioning
If I lacked anything.

'A guest', I answered, 'worthy to be here.'
Love said, 'You shall be he.'
'I, the unkind, ungrateful? Ah, my dear,
I cannot look on thee.'

Love took my hand, and smiling did reply,
'Who made the eyes but I?'

'Truth, Lord, but I have marred them, let my shame,
Go where, it doth deserve.'
'And know you not', says Love, 'who bore the blame?'
'My dear, then I will serve.'
'You must sit down', says Love,'and taste my meat.'
So I did sit and eat.

PICTURE • PONDER • PRAY • PROMISE

A PRAYER

Lord you love every part of us,
Even our shame and despair:
Help us believe in your love. Amen.

Pray for people whom you dislike, and
for those rejected because of race, creed, or colour,
because they lack 'respectability' or because of
their way of life.

Thank God that he loves and cares for all his creation.

Lord, to whom shall we go?
To you! For your love is eternal.
All praise to the God of heaven!
Praise him for ever!

O Lord, open our lips:
Let us praise you, Lord of Creation.
May the peace of the Lord rule our hearts:
For he calls us to love him for ever.

READING: A NEW TESTAMENT HYMN – COLOSSIANS 1: 15-16

Christ is the image of the invisible God,
He is the first born of all creation;
In him all things were created,
In heaven and on earth,
Visible and invisible,
All was created through him and for him.

READING: MARK 2:23-28

Jesus Teaches About the Sabbath

Jesus was walking through some cornfields on the Sabbath. As his disciples walked along with him, they began to pick the ears of corn. So the Pharisees said to Jesus, 'Look, it is against our Law for your disciples to do that on the Sabbath!'

Jesus answered, 'Have you never read what David did that time when he needed something to eat? He and his men were hungry, so he went into the house of God and ate the bread offered to God. This happened when Abiathar was the High Priest. According to our Law only the priests may eat this bread – but David ate it and even gave it to his men.'

And Jesus concluded, 'The Sabbath was made for the good of man; man was not made for the Sabbath. So the Son of Man is Lord even of the Sabbath.'

PICTURE · PONDER · PRAY · PROMISE

A PRAYER

> Lord of time and space,
> Lord of worlds known and unknown,
> Grant us the wisdom to see life through your eyes,
> And to let you lead us into all truth. Amen.

Pray for those who live cramped and boring lives,
> for those who fear change and development,
> for those who keep their religion for Sundays,
> for those who lack a vision of God.

Praise God that faith in Jesus makes us free of
conventionalism and slavery to wordly ambition.

Thank God that he is Lord of time and space.

> I am the first and the last, says the Lord:
> **The beginning and the end of creation.**
> Lord, whom else could we adore?
> **You are the Word of eternal life.**

O Lord, open our lips:
And our mouth shall proclaim your praise.
We will praise you, O Lord, with all our heart:
We will glorify your name forever.

READING: A CELTIC HYMN OF SELF-DEDICATION

Be thou my vision, beloved Lord:
King of the Seven Heavens.
Be thou in my thoughts day and night:
Even when I sleep.
Be thou in my speech:
Be thou my understanding.
Be thou for me that I may be all for thee.
Be thou my Father:
That I may be thy true child.
Thy love in my soul and my heart –
Grant this to me:
King of the Seven Heavens.
Beloved Christ: whatever befalls me:
Be thou my vision.

READING: MARK 3:13-27

Jesus Chooses the Twelve: Vocation and Controversy

Then Jesus went up a hill and called to himself the men he wanted. They came to him, and he chose twelve, whom he named apostles. 'I have chosen you to be with me,' he told them. 'I will also send you out to preach, and you will have authority to drive out demons.'

These are the twelve he chose: Simon (Jesus gave him the name Peter); James and his brother John, the sons of Zebedee (Jesus gave them the name Boanerges, which means 'Men of Thunder'); Andrew, Philip, Bartholomew, Matthew, Thomas, James son of Alphaeus, Thaddaeus, Simon the Patriot, and Judas Iscariot, who betrayed Jesus.

Then Jesus went home. Again such a large crowd gathered that Jesus and his disciples had no time to eat. When his family heard about it, they set out to take charge of him, because people were saying, 'He's gone mad!'

Some teachers of the Law who had come from Jerusalem were saying, 'He has Beelzebul in him! It is the chief of the demons who gives him the power to drive them out.'

So Jesus called them to him and spoke to them in parables: 'How can Satan drive out Satan? If a country divides itself into groups which fight each other, that country will fall apart: If a family divides itself into groups which fight each other, that family will fall apart. So if Satan's kingdom divides into groups, it cannot last, but will fall apart and come to an end.

'No one can break into a strong man's house and take away his belongings unless he first ties up the strong man; then he can plunder his house.'

PICTURE • PONDER • PRAY • PROMISE

A PRAYER

O God of eternal life and love,
You turn upside-down all our expectations,
With you nothing is impossible.
Fill us with the loyalty of your earliest disciples.
Make us able to do great things for you. Amen.

Thank God for the lives of the saints,
for saints alive today,
for those whom we admire in Christ.

Pray for courage to live in Christ's way,
for those persecuted by their faith,
for those who suffer ridicule because they believe.

Jesus calls us! By your mercies:
Saviour, may we hear your call.
Fill our hearts with true obedience:
To serve, to love you best of all.

'Be Thou My Vision', edited and translated by Gerald Murphy, is from *Early Irish Lyrics*, 1956, and is reproduced by permission of the publisher, Oxford University Press.

O Lord, open our ears to your truth:
And our lives shall proclaim your praise.
O give thanks to the Lord for his goodness:
For his mercy endures for ever.

READING: MARK 4:1-20

The Parable of the Sower

Again Jesus began to teach beside Lake Galilee. The crowd that gathered round him was so large that he got into a boat and sat in it. The boat was out in the water, and the crowd stood on the shore at the water's edge. He used parables to teach them many things, saying to them:

'Listen! Once there was a man who went out to sow corn. As he scattered the seed in the field, some of it fell along the path, and the birds came and ate it up. Some of it fell on rocky ground, where there was little soil. The seeds soon sprouted, because the soil wasn't deep. Then, when the sun came up, it burnt the young plants; and because the roots had not grown deep enough, the plants soon dried up. Some of the seed fell among thorn bushes, which grew up and choked the plants, and they didn't produce any corn. But some seeds fell in good soil, and the plants sprouted, grew, and produced corn: some had thirty grains, others sixty, and others a hundred.'

And Jesus concluded, 'Listen, then, if you have ears!'

When Jesus was alone, some of those who had heard him came to him with the twelve disciples and asked him to explain the parables. 'You have been given the secret of the Kingdom of God,' Jesus answered. 'But the others, who are on the outside, hear all things by means of parables, so that,

"They may look and look, yet not see;
they may listen and listen, yet not understand.

For if they did, they would turn to God,
and he would forgive them."'

Then Jesus asked them, 'Don't you understand this parable? How, then, will you ever understand any parable? The sower sows God's message. Some people are like the seeds that fall along the path; as soon as they hear the message, Satan comes and takes it away. Other people are like the seeds that fall on rocky ground. As soon as they hear the message, they receive it gladly. But it does not sink deep into them, and they don't last long. So when trouble or persecution comes because of the message, they give up at once. Other people are like the seeds sown among the thorn bushes. These are the ones who hear the message, but the worries about this life, the love for riches, and all other kinds of desires crowd in and choke the message, and they don't bear fruit. But other people are like the seeds sown in good soil. They hear the message, accept it, and bear fruit: some thirty, some sixty, and some a hundred.'

READING: LINES BY HARRY ALFORD AND OTHERS

All this world is God's own field,
Fruit unto his praise to yield;
Wheat and tares therein are sown,
Unto joy or sorrow grown;
Ripening with a wondrous power
Till the final harvest hour:
Grant, O Lord of life, that we
Holy grain and pure may be.

Come then, Lord of mercy, come,
Bid us sing thy harvest-home:
Let thy saints be gathered in,
Free from sorrow, free from sin;
All upon the heavenly floor
Praising thee for evermore:
Come, in all thy glory come,
Bid us sing thy harvest-home.

PICTURE · PONDER · PRAY · PROMISE

A Prayer

> Lord of Life and Father of Creation
> We thank you for the world in which we live,
> For the food you give us for soul as well as body.
> Grant that our lives may bring forth fruits of
>   holiness and love. Amen.

Thank God for his creation,
  for its beauty and bounty.

Pray for those suffering famine and poverty,
  for those starved of food and love by the
    cruelty and neglect of others.
  for those who strive for justice and for a
    fair distribution of the world's good things.
  for those who seek to share their spiritual, intellectual
    and artistic wealth with those whose horizons
    are cramped and boring.

> O bless our God, you nations;
> **Bless him in word and deed.**
> O bless our God all people;
> **Bless him by blessing others.**

O Lord, open our lips:
And our mouth shall proclaim your praise.
Our help comes from the Lord:
Who has made heaven and earth.

READING: PSALM 121

I lift up my eyes to the hills:
  But where shall I find help?
My help comes from the Lord:
  Who has made heaven and earth.
He will not suffer your foot to stumble:
  And he who watches over you will not sleep.
Be sure he who has charge of Israel:
  will neither slumber nor sleep.
The Lord himself is your keeper:
  The Lord is your defence upon your right hand;
The sun shall not strike you by day:
  Nor shall the moon by night.
The Lord will defend you from all evil:
  It is he who will guard your life.
The Lord will defend your going out
  and your coming in:
  From this time forward for evermore.

READING: MARK 4:35-41

Jesus, Lord of Nature

On the evening of that same day Jesus said to his
disciples, 'Let us go across to the other side of the lake.'
So they left the crowd; the disciples got into the boat in
which Jesus was already sitting, and they took him with
them. Other boats were there too. Suddenly a strong
wind blew up, and the waves began to spill over into the
boat, so that it was about to fill with water. Jesus was in
the back of the boat, sleeping with his head on a pillow.
The disciples woke him up and said, 'Teacher, don't you
care that we are about to die?'

Jesus stood up and commanded the wind, 'Be quiet!' and he said to the waves, 'Be still!' The wind died down, and there was a great calm. Then Jesus said to his disciples, 'Why are you frightened? Have you still no faith?'

But they were terribly afraid and said to one another, 'Who is this man? Even the wind and waves obey him!'

PICTURE • PONDER • PRAY • PROMISE

A PRAYER

Lord of Creation, Master of Time and Space,
We praise, we adore your greatness.
Help us to reverence the power and beauty of
  your creation, and to make wise use of your gifts.
Amen.

Pray for those who have no faith, no eye for beauty,
  no reverence for life.
Pray for those who are filled with fear at the forces
  of nature and the cleverness of mankind.

Let all things their Creator bless;
And worship him in humbleness.
O praise him!
Alleluia!

O Lord, open our lips:
To praise your power to save.
Our help is in the name of the Lord:
Creator of heaven and earth.

READING: PSALM 107:17-22

Fools were far gone in transgression:
    and because of their sins were afflicted.
They sickened at any food:
    and had come to the gates of death.
Then they cried to the Lord in their distress:
    and he took them out of their trouble.
He sent his word and healed them:
    and saved their life from the Pit.
Let them thank the Lord for his goodness:
    and for the wonders that he does for the
    children of men;
Let them offer sacrifices of thanksgiving:
    and tell what he has done with shouts of joy.

READING: MARK 5:1-20

Jesus, Healer of Mankind

Jesus and his disciples arrived on the other side of
Lake Galilee, in the territory of Gerasa. As soon as Jesus
got out of the boat, he was met by a man who came out
of the burial caves there. This man had an evil spirit in
him and lived among the tombs. Nobody could keep him
chained up any more; many times his feet and hands had
been chained, but every time he broke the chains and
smashed the irons on his feet. He was too strong for
anyone to control him. Day and night he wandered
among the tombs and through the hills, screaming and
cutting himself with stones.

He was some distance away when he saw Jesus; so he
ran, fell on his knees before him, and screamed in a loud

voice, 'Jesus, Son of the Most High God! What do you want with me? For God's sake, I beg you, don't punish me!' (He said this because Jesus was saying, 'Evil spirit, come out of this man!')

So Jesus asked him, 'What is your name?'

The man answered, 'My name is "Mob" – there are many of us!' And he kept begging Jesus not to send the evil spirits out of that region.

There was a large herd of pigs nearby, feeding on a hillside. So the spirits begged Jesus, 'Send us to the pigs, and let us go into them.' He let them go, and the evil spirits went out of the man and entered the pigs. The whole herd – about two thousand pigs in all – rushed down the side of the cliff into the lake and was drowned.

The men who had been taking care of the pigs ran away and spread the news in the town among the farms. People went out to see what had happened, and when they came to Jesus, they saw the man who used to have the mob of demons in him. He was sitting there, clothed and in his right mind; and they were all afraid.

Those who had seen it told the people what had happened to the man with the demons, and about the pigs.

So they asked Jesus to leave their territory.

As Jesus was getting into the boat, the man who had had the demons begged him, 'Let me go with you!'

But Jesus would not let him. Instead he told him, 'Go back home to your family and tell them how much the Lord has done for you and how kind he has been to you.'

So the man left and went all through the Ten Towns, telling what Jesus had done for him. And all who heard it were amazed.

PICTURE · PONDER · PRAY · PROMISE

A Prayer

Healer of the sorrows of mankind,
Turner of evil into good,
Saviour of all from all evil,
We praise and adore you for ever. Amen.

Praise and thank God who can save
and heal all who put their trust in him.

Pray for those in distress of mind and body,
and for those who care for them.

What seems to be God's foolishness:
Is wiser than human wisdom.
Lord, to whom shall we go?
You have the words of eternal life.

O Lord, open our lips:
To praise your healing power.
May your healing touch:
Transform our human lives.

READING: LINES BY J. G. WHITTIER

Our outward lips confess the Name
All other names above;
Love only knoweth whence it came,
And understandeth love.

We may not climb the heavenly steeps
To bring the Lord Christ down;
In vain we search the lowest deeps,
For him no depths can drown.

The healing of his seamless robe
Is by our beds of pain;
We touch him in life's throng and press,
And we are whole again.

Alone, O Love ineffable,
Thy saving name is given;
To turn aside from you is hell,
To walk with you is heaven.

READING: MARK 5:25-34

The Woman who Touched Jesus' Cloak

There was a woman who had suffered terribly from severe bleeding for twelve years, even though she had been treated by many doctors. She had spent all her money, but instead of getting better she got worse all the time. She had heard about Jesus, so she came in the crowd behind him, saying to herself, 'If I just touch his clothes, I will get well.'

She touched his cloak, and her bleeding stopped at once; and she had the feeling inside herself that she was healed of her trouble. At once Jesus knew that power had gone out of him, so he turned round in the crowd and asked, 'Who touched my clothes?'

His disciples answered, 'You see how the people are crowding you; why do you ask who touched you?'

But Jesus kept looking round to see who had done it. The woman realised what had happened to her, so she came, trembling with fear, knelt at his feet, and told him the whole truth. Jesus said to her, 'My daughter, your faith has made you well. Go in peace, and be healed of your trouble.'

PICTURE • PONDER • PRAY • PROMISE

A PRAYER

> God of love, sharer of human life,
> Become our touchstone and our Lord,
> To make us whole. Amen.

Praise God that faith can bring healing power
    into our lives.

Pray for the sick, and in particular those whose illness
    has been pronounced incurable.

> Your faith has made you well:
> **Go in peace.**
> God's love is always true:
> **Go in peace.**

O Lord, open our lips:
And our mouth shall proclaim your praise.
Let us be glad and rejoice in your name:
Your words are truth.

READING: MARK 6:1-6

Jesus is Rejected

Jesus left that place and went back to his home town, followed by his disciples. On the Sabbath he began to teach in the synagogue. Many people were there; and when they heard him, they were all amazed. 'Where did he get all this?' they asked. 'What wisdom is this that has been given him? How does he perform miracles? Isn't he the carpenter, the son of Mary, and the brother of James, Joseph, Judas, and Simon? Aren't his sisters living here?' And so they rejected him.

Jesus said to them, 'A prophet is respected everywhere except in his own home town and by his relatives and his family.'

He was not able to perform any miracles there, except that he placed his hands on a few sick people and healed them. He was greatly surprised, because the people did not have faith.

READING: LINES BY W. W. HOW

It is a thing most wonderful,
Almost too wonderful to be,
That God's own Son should come from heaven
And die to save a child like me.

And yet I know that it is true;
He chose a poor and humble lot,
And wept and toiled and mourned and died
For love of those who loved him not.

And yet I want to love thee, Lord!
O light the flame within my heart,

And I will love thee more and more,
Until I see thee as thou art.

PICTURE · PONDER · PRAY · PROMISE

A Prayer

> Lord, save us from prejudice of every kind.
> Open our eyes to truth wherever we may see it
> And make us love you more. Amen.

Praise God for Jesus, Lord of Truth,
> Saviour of the world.

Thank him for faith and pray to love him more.

Pray for people whom we take for granted.

Pray to see God in all people.

> Is not this the carpenter, the son of Mary?
> **Yet he is Emmanuel: God among us.**
> Lord, to whom shall we go for truth?
> **You have the words of eternal life.**

O Lord, open our lips:
And our mouth shall proclaim your praise.
Let our lives be lived in your truth:
And our hearts ever true to your love.

READING: 'SIR JOHN THE BAPTIST' BY SIDNEY KEYES

I, John, not reed but root;
Not vested priest nor saviour but a voice
Crying daylong like a cricket in the heat,
Demand your worship. Not of me
But of the traveller I am calling
From beyond Jordan and the limestone hills,
Whose runner and rude servant I am only.
Not man entirely but God's watchman,
I dwell among these blistered rocks
Awaiting the wide dawn, the wonder
Of his first coming, and the Dove's descent.

READING: MARK 6:14-29

The Killing of John the Baptist

Now King Herod heard about all this, because Jesus' reputation had spread everywhere. Some people were saying, 'John the Baptist has come back to life! That is why he has this power to perform miracles.'

Others, however, said, 'He is Elijah.' Others said, 'He is a prophet, like one of the prophets of long ago.'

When Herod heard it, he said, 'He is John the Baptist! I had his head cut off, but he has come back to life!' Herod himself had ordered John's arrest, and he had him chained and put in prison. Herod did this because of Herodias, whom he had married, even though she was the wife of his brother Philip. John the Baptist kept telling Herod, 'It isn't right for you to be married to your brother's wife!'

So Herodias held a grudge against John and wanted to kill him, but she could not because of Herod. Herod was afraid of John, because he knew that John was a good and holy man, and so he kept him safe. He liked to listen to him, even though he became greatly disturbed every time he heard him.

Finally, Herodias got her chance. It was on Herod's birthday. when he gave a feast for all the chief government officials, the military commanders, and the leading citizens of Galilee. The daughter of Herodias came in and danced, and pleased Herod and his guests. So the king said to the girl, 'What would you like to have? I will give you anything you want.' With many vows he said to her, 'I swear that I will give you anything you ask for, even as much as half my kingdom!'

So the girl went out and asked her mother, 'What shall I ask for?'

'The head of John the Baptist', she answered.

The girl hurried back at once to the king and demanded, 'I want you to give me here and now the head of John the Baptist on a dish!'

This made the king very sad, but he could not refuse her because of all the vows he had made in front of all his guests.

So he sent off a guard at once with orders to bring John's head. The guard left, went to the prison, and cut John's head off; then he brought it on a dish and gave it to the girl, who gave it to her mother. When John's disciples heard about this, they came and took away his body, and buried it.

PICTURE · PONDER · PRAY · PROMISE

A Prayer

Lord, as your servant John the Baptist
  was killed for his witness to truth:
Give us courage to defend all that is good and
  true. Amen.

Praise God for moral truth and pray to be true to it.

Thank God that he trusts us to speak truth.

Pray for people consumed by hatred and revenge.

Pray for willingness to forgive and be forgiven.

God grant us grace to follow his saints:
In faith and hope and love.
God is love:
May we abide in love for ever.

'Sir John the Baptist' by Sidney Keyes is from *Collected Poems*, and is reproduced by permission of the publisher, Routledge.

O Lord, open our lips:
To praise you in love and in truth.
Fill our minds and our bodies with light:
That our lives shall be wholly for you.

READING: PSALM 1

Blessed is the man who has not walked
   in the counsel of the ungodly:
   nor followed the way of sinners
   nor taken his seat amongst the scornful.

But his delight is in the law of the Lord:
   and on that law will he ponder day and night.

He is like a tree planted beside streams of water:
   that yields its fruit in due season.

Its leaves also shall not wither:
   and look whatever he does it shall prosper.

As for the ungodly it is not so with them:
   they are like the chaff which the wind scatters.

Therefore the ungodly shall not stand up at the judgement:
   nor sinners in the congregation of the righteous.

For the Lord cares for the way of the righteous:
   but the way of the ungodly shall perish.

READING: MARK 7:1-13

Jesus Speaks about Integrity

Some Pharisees and teachers of the Law who had come from Jerusalem gathered round Jesus. They noticed that some of his disciples were eating their food with hands that were ritually unclean – that is, they had not washed them in the way the Pharisees said people should.

(For the Pharisees, as well as the rest of the Jews, follow the teaching they received from their ancestors: they do not eat unless they wash their hands in the proper way; nor do they eat anything that comes from the market unless they wash it first. And they follow many other rules which they have received, such as the proper way to wash cups, pots, copper bowls and beds.)

So the Pharisees and the teachers of the Law asked Jesus, 'Why is it that your disciples do not follow the teaching handed down by our ancestors, but instead eat with ritually unclean hands?'

Jesus answered them, 'How right Isaiah was when he prophesied about you! You are hypocrites, just as he wrote:

"These people, says God, honour me with their words,
but their heart is really far away from me.
It is no use for them to worship me, because they
teach man-made rules as though they were
God's laws!"

'You put aside God's command and obey the teachings of men.'

And Jesus continued, 'You have a clever way of rejecting God's law in order to uphold your own teaching. For Moses commanded, "Respect your father and your mother" and, "Whoever curses his father or mother is to be put to death."

But you teach that if a person has something he could use to help his father or mother, but says, "This is Corban" (which means, it belongs to God), he is excused from helping his father or mother. In this way the teaching you pass on to others cancels out the word of God. And there are many other things like this that you do.'

PICTURE · PONDER · PRAY · PROMISE

A Prayer

Jesus, you are the way, the life that is whole and true:
Help us to follow your way. Amen.

Praise God that Jesus shows what is truth in a world
of confusion.

Pray to be consistent, to have oneness in mind and spirit.

Pray for those whose work is in journalism
and broadcasting.

Make our hearts clean, O Lord:
Renew a right spirit within us.
In singleness of heart:
May we live in the way of eternal life.

O Lord, open our lips:
To praise you in words that are pure.
Teach us to know what is good:
And give us the strength to achieve it.

READING: LINES BY JOHN KEBLE

Blest are the pure in heart,
For they shall see our God,
The secret of the Lord is theirs,
Their soul is Christ's abode.

The Lord, who left the heavens
Our life and peace to bring,
To dwell in lowliness with men,
Their pattern and their King;

Still to the lowly soul
He doth himself impart,
And for his dwelling and his throne
Chooseth the pure in heart.

Lord, we thy presence seek;
May ours this blessing be;
Give us a pure and lowly heart,
A temple meet for thee.

READING: MARK 7:14-23

Jesus Explains True Purity of Heart

Then Jesus called the crowd to him once more and said to them, 'Listen to me, all of you, and understand. There is nothing that goes into a person from the outside which can make him ritually unclean. Rather it is what comes out of a person that makes him unclean.'

When he left the crowd and went into the house, his disciples asked him to explain this saying. 'You are no more intelligent than the others,' Jesus said to them, 'Don't you understand? Nothing that goes into a person from the outside can make him unclean, because it does not go into his heart but into his stomach and then goes on out of the body.' (In saying this, Jesus declared that all foods are fit to be eaten.)

And he went on to say, 'It is what comes out of a person that makes him unclean. For from the inside, from a person's heart, come the evil ideas which lead him to do immoral things, to rob, kill, commit adultery, be greedy, and do all sorts of evil things; deceit, indecency, jealousy, slander, pride and folly – all these evil things come from inside a person and make him unclean.'

PICTURE • PONDER • PRAY • PROMISE

A PRAYER

> Heal our souls and minds, God our Creator:
> We thank you for your love,
> May we live in the power of your Spirit. Amen.

Thank God that he knows us through and through.

Pray for grace to admit our faults,
  and receive his demanding forgiveness.

Pray for those who do not believe in God's way,
  that they shall be liberated from guilt.

> Create in me a clean heart O God:
> **And renew a right spirit within me.**
> Do not cast me out from your presence:
> **Do not take your holy spirit from me.**
> O give me the gladness of your help again:
> **and support me with a willing spirit.**
>
> *Psalm 51:10-12*

O Lord, open our lips:
To praise you, the Lord of all healing.
O God, make speed to save us:
O Lord, make haste to heal us.

READING: MARK 7:24-30

Jesus Responds to an Act of Faith

Then Jesus left and went away to the territory near the city of Tyre. He went into a house and did not want anyone to know that he was there, but he could not stay hidden. A woman, whose daughter had an evil spirit in her, heard about Jesus and came to him at once and fell at his feet. The woman was a Gentile, born in the region of Phoenicia in Syria. She begged Jesus to drive the demon out of her daughter. But Jesus answered, 'Let us first feed the children. It isn't right to take the children's food and throw it to the dogs.'

'Sir,' she answered, 'even the dogs under the table eat the children's leftovers!'

So Jesus said to her, 'Because of that answer, go back home, where you will find that the demon has gone out of your daughter!'

She went home and found her child lying on the bed; the demon had indeed gone out of her.

READING: PSALM 116:4-9

I called upon the name of the Lord:
  'O Lord, I beseech you, deliver me!'
Gracious and righteous is the Lord:
  full of compassion is our God.
The Lord preserves the simple:
  when I was brought low he saved me.
Return O my soul to your rest:
  for the Lord has rewarded you.

For you O Lord have delivered my soul from death:
    My eyes from tears and my feet from falling.
I will walk before the Lord:
    In the land of the living.

PICTURE • PONDER • PRAY • PROMISE

A Prayer

    Praise to you, O God our loving King,
    For you love all your human children;
    Help us to trust and to love you. Amen.

Praise God for his love of all people, of every race,
    of every century.

Thank him for health and pray for those who are sick.

Pray for those who have no-one to pray for them.

Pray for doctors, surgeons, and all health workers,
    especially for those who help us personally.

    Lord, we believe:
    Make good our belief!
    Let us walk in your strength:
    Every day of our lives.

O Lord, open our lips:
To praise you with understanding.
Give us the freedom of truth:
To see life through your eyes and your life.

READING: PSALM 119:97-104

Lord how I love your law:
  it is my meditation all the day long.
Your commandments have made me wiser than
    my enemies:
  for they remain with me for ever.
I have more understanding than all my teachers:
  for I study your commands.
I am wiser than the aged:
  because I have kept your precepts.
I have held back my feet from every evil path:
  that I might keep your word.
I have not turned aside from your judgements:
  for you yourself are my teacher.
How sweet are your words to my tongue:
  sweeter than honey to my mouth.
Through your precepts I get understanding:
  therefore I hate all lying ways.

READING: MARK 8:11-21

Jesus Not Understood

Some Pharisees came to Jesus and started to argue
with him. They wanted to trap him, so they asked him to
perform a miracle to show that God approved of him.
But Jesus gave a deep groan and said, 'Why do the
people of this day ask for a miracle? No, I tell you! No
such proof will be given to these people!'

He left them, got back into the boat, and started across to the other side of the lake.

The disciples had forgotten to bring enough bread and had only one loaf with them in the boat. 'Take care,' Jesus warned them, 'and be on your guard against the yeast of the Pharisees and the yeast of Herod.'

They started discussing among themselves: 'He says this because we haven't any bread.'

Jesus knew what they were saying so he asked them, 'Why are you discussing about not having any bread? Don't you know or understand yet? Are your minds so dull? You have eyes – can't you see? You have ears – can't you hear? Don't you remember when I broke the five loaves for the five thousand people? How many baskets full of leftover pieces did you take up?'

'Twelve,' they answered.

'And when I broke the seven loaves for the four thousand people,' asked Jesus, 'how many baskets full of leftover pieces did you take up?'

'Seven', they answered.

'And you still don't understand?' he asked them.

PICTURE · PONDER · PRAY · PROMISE

A PRAYER

O God, Father, Son and Holy Spirit:
Make us sensitive to your presence in the
daily life we live. Amen.

Thank God for the beauty, subtlety and power of
his creation,

Pray for those who have no faith.

Pray for those who reject faith without understanding.

Pray for grace to share our faith in ways that others can understand.

Christ is God's light for all
May we follow his way for ever.
He is the light of the world:
May the nations be healed by his truth.

O Lord, open our lips:
To praise you as Saviour and Lord.
May Jesus the true Messiah:
Make us whole by his death on the cross.

READING: MARK 8:27-9:1

Jesus and Peter

Then Jesus and his disciples went away to the villages near Caesarea Philippi. On the way he asked them 'Tell me, who do people say I am?'

'Some say that you are John the Baptist,' they answered; 'others say that you are Elijah, while others say that you are one of the prophets.'

'What about you?' he asked them. 'Who do you say I am?'

Peter answered, 'You are the Messiah.'

Then Jesus ordered them, 'Do not tell anyone about me.'

Then Jesus began to teach his disciples: 'The Son of Man must suffer much and be rejected by the elders, the chief priests and the teachers of the Law. He will be put to death, but three days later he will rise to life.' He made this very clear to them. So Peter took him aside and began to rebuke him. But Jesus turned round, looked at his disciples, and rebuked Peter. 'Get away from me, Satan,' he said. 'Your thoughts don't come from God but from man!'

Then Jesus called the crowd and his disciples to him. 'If anyone wants to come with me,' he told them, 'he must forget self, carry his cross, and follow me. For whoever wants to save his own life will lose it; but whoever loses his life for me and for the gospel will save it. Does a person gain anything if he wins the whole world but loses his life? Of course not! There is nothing he can give to regain his life. If a person is ashamed of me and of my teaching in this godless and wicked day, then the Son of Man will be ashamed of him when he comes in the glory of his Father with the holy angels.'

And he went on to say, 'I tell you, there are some here who will not die until they have seen the Kingdom of God come with power.'

READING: LINES BY C. W. EVEREST

'Take up thy cross,' the Saviour said,
'If thou wouldst my disciple be;
Deny thyself, the world forsake,
And humbly follow after me.'

Take up thy cross, and follow Christ,
Nor think till death to lay it down;
For only he who bears the cross
May hope to wear the glorious crown.

PICTURE • PONDER • PRAY • PROMISE

A PRAYER

Lord of life and death,
   the Christ who is saving the world:
Help us to understand the glory of your cross,
   to find life in you. Amen.

Thank God for Peter's realisation of Jesus' Messiahship.

Pray for wholeness of understanding and for faith that endures as well as rejoices.

Pray to be free from self-deceit, and for all who live in worlds of fantasy.

Pray for those who deceive others.

Jesus is Messiah:
Alleluia!
He calls us to carry his cross:
To share in his conquest of death!

Let us worship the Lord:
All praise to his name.
O Lord, open our hearts:
To adore you in all your glory.

READING: MARK 9:2-9

Jesus Transfigured in Glory

Six days later Jesus took with him Peter, James and John, and led them up a high mountain, where they were alone. As they looked on, a change came over Jesus, and his clothes became shining white – whiter than anyone in the world could wash them. Then the three disciples saw Elijah and Moses talking with Jesus. Peter spoke up and said to Jesus, 'Teacher, how good it is that we are here! We will make three tents, one for you, one for Moses, and one for Elijah.' He and the others were so frightened that he did not know what to say.

Then a cloud appeared and covered them with its shadow, and a voice came from the cloud, 'This is my own dear Son – listen to him!' They took a quick look round but did not see anyone else; only Jesus was with them.

As they came down the mountain, Jesus ordered them, 'Don't tell anyone what you have seen, until the Son of Man has risen from death.'

READING: LINES BY CHARLES WESLEY

Rejoice! the Lord is King!
Your Lord and King adore;
Mortals give thanks and sing,
And triumph evermore:

His kingdom cannot fail;
He rules o'er earth and heaven;
The keys of death and hell
Are to our Jesus given:

Lift up your heart, lift up your voice;
Rejoice, again I say, rejoice!

PICTURE • PONDER • PRAY • PROMISE

A PRAYER

> Lord, as we go about the details of our daily lives,
> Help us remember that you are our Lord
>   and our God. Amen.

Praise and thank God that Jesus unites heaven and earth;
that in Jesus we know God in all truth.

Pray for people whose vision of life leaves out God.

Pray for evangelists and pray to be able to share faith
with others.

> Christ is God's own dear Son:
> **Let us listen to him.**
> He is the Son of Man:
> **Who has conquered evil and death.**

O Lord, open our lips:
In prayer that proclaims your power.
Our faith may be never enough:
But you can complete us in faith.

READING: MARK 9:14-29

Jesus Succeeds where his Followers have Failed

When they joined the rest of the disciples, they saw a large crowd round them and some teachers of the Law arguing with them. When the people saw Jesus, they were greatly surprised, and ran to him and greeted him. Jesus asked his disciples, 'What are you arguing with them about?'

A man in the crowd answered, 'Teacher, I brought my son to you, because he has an evil spirit in him and cannot talk. Whenever the spirit attacks him, it throws him to the ground, and he foams at the mouth, grits his teeth, and becomes stiff all over. I asked your disciples to drive the spirit out, but they could not.'

Jesus said to them, 'How unbelieving you people are! How long must I stay with you? How long do I have to put up with you? Bring the boy to me!' They brought him to Jesus.

As soon as the spirit saw Jesus, it threw the boy into a fit, so that he fell on the ground and rolled round, foaming at the mouth. 'How long has he been like this?' Jesus asked the father.

'Ever since he was a child,' he replied. 'Many times the evil spirit has tried to kill him by throwing him in the fire and into water. Have pity on us and help us, if you possibly can!'

'Yes,' said Jesus, 'if you yourself can! Everything is possible for the person who has faith.'

The father at once cried out 'I do have faith, but not enough. Help me to have more!'

Jesus noticed that the crowd was closing in on them, so he gave a command to the evil spirit. 'Deaf and dumb spirit,' he said, 'I order you to come out of the boy and never go into him again!'

The spirit screamed, threw the boy into a bad fit, and came out. The boy looked like a corpse, and everyone said 'He is dead!' But Jesus took the boy by the hand and helped him to rise, and he stood up.

After Jesus had gone indoors, his disciples asked him privately, 'Why couldn't we drive the spirit out ?'

'Only prayer can drive this kind out,' Jesus answered, 'nothing else can.'

READING: 'THE FAITH CAME FIRST' BY SIDNEY CARTER

The faith came first.
In the beginning was
the way that I believe
and after that
came all that I believe in.

Hitler, Christ,
Apollo, Aphrodite
and Karl Marx
fruit, thorn or flower
on a single tree.
Faith is the sap of it.

By faith I test
the gospel of St Matthew,
Michelangelo,
Bach or the Beatles
but
the faith came first, I see
no other rock
but this to
build upon.

PICTURE • PONDER • PRAY • PROMISE

A Prayer

> Father, Spirit, Son: One living God;
> Transform the weakness of our faith,
> And teach us how to pray. Amen.

Thank God for your faith, however weak it may feel to you.

Pray to grow stronger in the art of prayer.

Pray for those who seem beyond healing.

> Lord, we believe:
> **Yet heal our unbelief**
> Lord, we want to love you more:
> **So light the fire of love in our hearts.**

'The Faith came first' by Sydney Carter, is from *The Two-way clock*, and is reproduced by permission of the publisher, Stainer & Bell Ltd.

O Lord, open our lips:
To praise you who suffered for us.
You are in all mankind:
Teach us to see you in others.

READING: MARK 9:30-41

Jesus describes true greatness as service of others

Jesus and his disciples left that place and went on through Galilee. Jesus did not want anyone to know where he was, because he was teaching his disciples: 'The Son of Man will be handed over to men who will kill him. Three days later, however, he will rise to life.'

But they did not understand what this teaching meant, and they were afraid to ask him.

They came to Capernaum, and after going indoors Jesus asked his disciples, 'What were you arguing about on the road?'

But they would not answer him, because on the road they had been arguing among themselves about who was the greatest. Jesus sat down, called the twelve disciples, and said to them, 'Whoever wants to be first must place himself last of all and be the servant of all.' Then he took a child and made him stand in front of them. He put his arms round him and said to them, 'Whoever welcomes in my name one of these children, welcomes me: and whoever welcomes me, welcomes not only me but also the one who sent me.'

John said to him, 'Teacher, we saw a man who was driving out demons in your name, and we told him to stop, because he doesn't belong to our group.'

'Do not try to stop him,' Jesus told them, 'because no-one who performs a miracle in my name will be able soon afterwards to say evil things about me. For whoever is not against us is for us. I assure you that anyone who gives you a drink of water because you belong to me will certainly receive his reward.'

READING: 'INCOGNITO' BY GILES AMBROSE

We find thee, Lord, in others' need
   We see thee in our brothers;
By loving word and kindly deed
   We serve the Man for Others.

We look around and see thy face
   Disfigured, marred, neglected;
We find thee Lord in every place,
   Sought for and unexpected.

We offer in simplicity
   Our loving gift and labour;
And what we do, we do to thee,
   Incarnate in our neighbour.

We love since we are loved by thee;
   New strength from thee we gather;
And in thy service we shall be
   Made perfect in each other.

PICTURE · PONDER · PRAY · PROMISE

A PRAYER

   Lord you have shown us in Jesus
      that true greatness is serving others:
   Help us to have the same love
      that we see in him. Amen.

Praise God for Jesus, for love and true greatness.

Thank him for opportunities to serve him in others.

Thank him for those who serve your daily needs
  in the community and in your home life.

Pray for the gift of intelligent compassion.

Pray for children and parents, especially those in trouble.

> Whoever would be first:
> **Must be last and servant of all.**
> Lord, may we welcome you:
> **In the people whom you have made.**

'Incognito' by Giles Ambrose, is reproduced by permission of the Society of the Sacred Mission.

O Lord, open our lips:
To praise you, the Father who loves us.
We are your children:
Free us from hardness of heart.

READING: LINES FROM 'ONLY MAN' BY D.H. LAWRENCE

Only man can fall from God
Only man.
No animal, no beast nor creeping thing
no cobra nor hyena nor scorpion
nor hideous white ant
can slip entirely through the fingers of
   the hands of God
into the abyss of self-knowledge,
Knowledge of the self-apart-from-God.

For the knowledge of the self-apart-from-God
is an abyss down which the soul can slip . . .
neither can it reach the depth
for the depth is bottomless,
so it wriggles its way even further down . . .
at last in sheer horror of not being able
   to leave off
knowing itself, knowing itself
   apart from God, falling.

READING: MARK 10:1-16

Jesus Speaks of the Kingdom of God

Then Jesus left that-place, went to the province of Judaea, and crossed the River Jordan. Crowds came flocking to him again, and he taught them, as he always did.

Some Pharisees came to him and tried to trap him. 'Tell us,' they asked, 'does our Law allow a man to divorce his wife?'

Jesus answered with a question, 'What law did Moses give you?'

Their answer was, 'Moses gave permission for a man to write a divorce notice and send his wife away.'

Jesus said to them, 'Moses wrote this law for you because you are so hard to teach. But in the beginning, at the time of creation, 'God made them male and female,' as the scripture says. "And for this reason a man will leave his father and mother and unite with his wife, and the two will become one." So they are no longer two, but one. Man must not separate, then, what God has joined together.'

When they went back into the house, the disciples asked Jesus about this matter. He said to them, 'A man who divorces his wife and marries another woman commits adultery against his wife. In the same way, a woman who divorces her husband and marries another man commits adultery.'

Some people brought children to Jesus for him to place his hands on them, but the disciples scolded the people.

When Jesus noticed this, he was angry and said to the disciples, 'Let the children come to me, and do not stop them, because the Kingdom of God belongs to such as these. I assure you that whoever does not receive the Kingdom of God like a child will never enter it.' Then he took the children in his arms, placed his hands on each of them, and blessed them.

PICTURE · PONDER · PRAY · PROMISE

A PRAYER:

O God you have made mankind
to live in human families.
Strengthen us all in the ways of fidelity
and tender love. Amen.

Praise God for all that is good in family life.

Pray for your own family.

Pray for those without family and friends.

Pray for those who work for the good of families,
for ourselves, teachers and for all who seek
to strengthen family life.

> Lord, your commands are hard:
> **to keep them we pray for your grace.**
> You are loving in all your ways:
> **and true in all your judgements.**

'Only Man' by D.H. Lawrence, is from Complete Poems and is reproduced by
permission of the publisher, Messrs Laurence Pollinger, the Estate of
Mrs Frieda Lawrence, and William Heinemann Ltd.

O Lord, open our lips:
To praise you, the King of Creation.
You teach us true goodness of heart:
Give us strength to become your true friends.

READING: MARK 10:17-31

Jesus Defines Eternal Prosperity

As Jesus was starting on his way again, a man ran up, knelt before him, and asked him, 'Good Teacher, what must I do to receive eternal life?'

'Why do you call me good?' Jesus asked him. 'No one is good except God alone. You know the commandments: "Do not commit murder; do not commit adultery; do not steal; do not accuse anyone falsely; do not cheat; respect your father and your mother."'

'Teacher,' the man said, 'ever since I was young, I have obeyed all these commandments.'

Jesus looked straight at him with love and said, 'You need only one thing. Go and sell all you have and give the money to the poor, and you will have riches in heaven; then come and follow me.' When the man heard this, gloom spread over his face, and he went away sad, because he was very rich.

Jesus looked round at his disciples and said to them, 'How hard it will be for rich people to enter the Kingdom of God!'

The disciples were shocked at these words, but Jesus went on to say, 'My children, how hard it is to enter the Kingdom of God! It is much harder for a rich man to enter the Kingdom of God than for a camel to go through the eye of a needle.'

At this the disciples were completely amazed and asked one another, 'Who, then, can be saved?'

Jesus looked straight at them and answered, 'This is impossible for man, but not for God; everything is possible for God.'

Then Peter spoke up, 'Look, we have left everything and followed you.'

'Yes', Jesus said to them, 'and I tell you that anyone who leaves home or brothers or sisters or mother or father or children or fields for me and for the gospel, will receive much more in this present age. He will receive a hundred times more houses, brothers, sisters, mothers, children and fields – and persecutions as well; and in the age to come he will receive eternal life. But many who now are first will be last, and many who now are last will be first.'

READING: LINES FROM 'ROCK OF AGES' BY A. M. TOPLADY

Rock of ages, cleft for me,
Let me hide myself in thee;
Let the water and the blood,
From thy riven side which flowed,
Be of sin the double cure:
Cleanse me from its guilt and power.

Nothing in my hand I bring,
Simply to the Cross I cling.

PICTURE · PONDER · PRAY · PROMISE

A PRAYER

Father eternal, God of the universe.
Deepen our loyalty,
Widen our love,
Help us to make you the first in our hearts. Amen.

Praise God who can give new life and love to all who
seek him through Jesus

Pray for those besotted by wealth and ambition.

Pray for those who suffer because of other
people's greed.

Pray for the starving and homeless, and for the rich
nations whose wealth can help them.

> Lord, how hard it is for the rich to enter
>   your Kingdom!
> **So make us aware of our poverty of spirit.**
> Lord, everything is possible to you:
> **By your grace we can follow your way.**

O Lord, open our lips:
To praise you, our Servant and King.
May your mind be in us:
And your praise on the lips of mankind.

READING: A NEW TESTAMENT HYMN: PHILIPPIANS 2:5-11 (RSV)

Have this mind among yourselves:
Which is yours in Christ Jesus.
Though he was in the form of God:
He did not grasp at equality with God,
But emptied himself.
Taking the form of a servant,
He was born in the likeness of men.
Being found in human form:
He humbled himself and became obedient unto death,
Even death on a cross.
Therefore God has highly exalted him,
And bestowed on him the name above every name,
That at the name of Jesus, every knee shall bow,
In heaven and on earth and under the earth.
Every tongue shall confess that Jesus Christ is Lord,
To the glory of God the Father.

READING: MARK 10:35-45

Jesus Speaks about True Greatness

Then James and John, the sons of Zebedee, came to Jesus.

'Teacher,' they said, 'there is something we want you to do for us.'

'What is it?' Jesus asked them.

They answered, 'When you sit on your throne in your glorious Kingdom, we want you to let us sit with you, one at your right hand and one at your left.'

Jesus said to them, 'You don't know what you are asking for. Can you drink the cup of suffering that I must drink? Can you be baptised in the way I must be baptised?'

'We can,' they answered.

Jesus said to them, 'You will indeed drink the cup I must drink and be baptized in the way I must be baptized. But I do not have the right to choose who will sit at my right and my left. It is God who will give these places to those for whom he has prepared them.'

When the other ten disciples heard about it, they became angry with James and John. So Jesus called them all together to him and said, 'You know that the men who are considered rulers of the heathen have power over them, and the leaders have complete authority. This, however, is not the way it is among you. If one of you wants to be great, he must be the servant of the rest: and if one of you wants to be first, he must be the slave of all. For even the Son of Man did not come to be served; he came to serve and to give his life to redeem many people.'

PICTURE • PONDER • PRAY • PROMISE

A PRAYER

Father, we praise and thank you
    for Jesus your Son who became the
    servant of all mankind to save us
    from evil and death;

By the power of the Holy Spirit
    may we serve you and all your creation. Amen

Thank God for Jesus.

Thank God that we are saved from evil and eternal death.

Pray for all who serve our daily needs.

Pray for grace to embrace suffering in God's service.

    The Son of Man came not to be served:
    But to serve
    He gave his life:
    To save us from sin and death.
    'You will drink my cup', he said:
    By his grace alone we shall live.

O Lord, open our lips:
Let us praise you with joy!
Blessed is he who comes in the name of the Lord:
Hosanna in the highest!

READING: MARK 11:1-10

Jesus Enters Jerusalem in Triumph

As they approached Jerusalem, near the towns of
Bethphage and Bethany, they came to the Mount of
Olives. Jesus sent two of his disciples on ahead with
these instructions: 'Go to the village there ahead of you.
As soon as you get there, you will find a colt tied up that
has never been ridden. Untie it and bring it here. And if
someone asks why you are doing that, tell him that the
Master needs it and will send it back at once.'

So they went and found a colt out in the street, tied to
the door of a house. As they were untying it, some of the
bystanders asked them, 'What are you doing, untying
that colt?'

They answered just as Jesus had told them, and the
men let them go. They brought the colt to Jesus, threw
their cloaks over the animal, and Jesus got on. Many
people spread their cloaks on the road, while others cut
branches in the fields and spread them on the road. The
people who were in front and those who followed
behind began to shout, 'Praise God! God bless him who
comes in the name of the Lord! God bless the coming
kingdom of King David, our father! Praise God!'

READING: LINES FROM 'THE DONKEY'S OWNER'

Snaffled my donkey, he did – good luck to him! –
Rode him astride, feet dangling, near scraping
   the ground.
Him and my little donkey! Ha! – laugh? –
I thought I'd kill myself when he first started.

So did the rest of them. Gave him a cheer
Like he was Caesar himself, only more hearty:
Tore off some palm-twigs and followed shouting,
Whacking the donkey's behind. . . .Then suddenly
We see his face.
The smile had gone, and somehow the way he sat
Was different – like he was much older – you know –
Didn't want to laugh no more.

PICTURE • PONDER • PRAY • PROMISE

A Prayer

Jesus our Lord,
you entered the city astride a donkey,
a King coming in peace:
May we share your joyful peace with all people. Amen.

Praise God for happiness.

Praise him for the confidence and joy of faith.

Pray for the peace of mind which comes from God alone.

Pray for those who have no peace of mind
for the anxious,
for the mentally sick,
for those who lack hope and faith.

Blessed be the God of Creation!
Let the world know the power of his love.
Blessed be Jesus our Lord!
Let the world be set free from sin.
Blessed be the Spirit of Life!
Let his fire renew our lives.

'The Donkey's Owner', by Clive Sansom, from *The Witnesses and Other Poems* and is reproduced by permission of the publisher, Methuen & Co. Ltd.

O Lord, open our lips:
To praise you in faith and obedience.
You have shown us the way of life:
Your service is perfect freedom.

READING: PSALM 118:19-24

Open me the gates of righteousness:
    and I will enter and give thanks to the Lord.

This is the gate of the Lord:
    the righteous shall enter it.

I will praise you for you answered me:
    and have become my salvation.

The stone that the builders rejected:
    has become the head of the corner.

This is the Lord's doing:
    and it is marvellous in our eyes.

This is the day that the Lord has made:
    let us rejoice and be glad in it.

READING: MARK 12:1-12

Jesus Utters a Solemn Warning

Then Jesus spoke to them in parables: 'Once there was a man who planted a vineyard, put a fence round it, dug a hole for the winepress, and built a watch-tower. Then he let out the vineyard to tenants and left home on a journey. When the time came to gather the grapes, he sent a slave to the tenants to receive from them his share of the harvest. The tenants seized the slave, beat him, and sent him back without a thing. Then the owner sent another slave; the tenants beat him over the head and treated him shamefully. The owner sent another slave, and they killed him; and they treated many others in the same way, beating some and killing others. The only one left to send was the man's own dear son. Last of all, then, he sent his son to the tenants. "I am sure they will respect my son," he said. But those tenants said to one another, "This is the owner's son. Come on, let's kill him, and his property will be ours!" So they seized the son and killed him and threw his body out of the vineyard.

'What, then, will the owner of the vineyard do?' asked Jesus. 'He will come and kill those men and hand the vineyard over to other tenants. Surely you have read this scripture?

"The stone which the builders rejected as worthless
    turned out to be the most important of all.
This was done by the Lord;
    what a wonderful sight it is!"'

The Jewish leaders tried to arrest Jesus, because they knew that he had told this parable against them. But they were afraid of the crowd, so they left him and went away.

PICTURE • PONDER • PRAY • PROMISE

A PRAYER

Lord, you know fear and the hatred
    that corrupts the human soul:

Lord, you expected your rejection
    and the cross:

Make us true to you in times of stress and danger,
    help us keep faith with you. Amen.

Thank God for all you have
    property
    cash
    friends and family.

Pray for deep awareness that what you have is his
    a gift from him
    a trust to be used for him.

Pray for those who have less than they need
   the homeless
   the starving
   refugees
   the neglected, especially children.

   Christ is our corner-stone:
   On him alone we build.
   The stone rejected by mankind:
   Is Jesus, on whom we rely.

O Lord, open our lips:
To praise you the God of life.
God is not God of the dead:
But of the living.

READING: MARK 12:18-27

Jesus Confounds the Sceptics

Then some Sadducees, who say that people will not rise from death, came to Jesus and said, 'Teacher, Moses wrote this law for us: "If a man dies and leaves a wife but no children, that man's brother must marry the widow so that they can have children who will be considered the dead man's children". Once there were seven brothers; the eldest got married and died without having children. Then the second one married the woman, and he also died without having children. The same thing happened to the third brother, and then to the rest: all seven brothers married the woman and died without having children. Last of all, the woman died. Now, when all the dead rise to life on the day of resurrection, whose wife will she be? All seven of them had married her.'

Jesus answered them. 'How wrong you are! And do you know why? It is because you don't know the Scriptures or God's power. For when the dead rise to life, they will be like the angels in heaven and will not marry. Now, as for the dead being raised: haven't you read in the book of Moses the passage about the burning bush? There it is written that God said to Moses, "I am the God of Abraham, the God of Isaac, and the God of Jacob." He is the God of the living, not of the dead. You are completely wrong!'

Reading: Psalm 107:17-22

Fools were far gone in transgression:
    and because of their sins were afflicted.

They sickened at any food:
    and had come to the gates of death.

Then they cried to the Lord in their distress:
    and he took them out of their trouble.

He sent his word and healed them:
    and saved their life from the Pit.

Let them thank the Lord for his goodness:
    and for the wonders that he does for the children
        of men.

Let them offer sacrifices of thanksgiving:
    and tell them what he has done with shouts of joy.

PICTURE · PONDER · PRAY · PROMISE

A Prayer

Lord of eternal life,
Raise us from the death of despair
And the tomb of unbelief:
May we live with you,
Both here and in eternity. Amen.

Thank God that he has given us eternal life.

Thank him that Jesus has conquered evil and death.

Pray for those who fear death,
    their own
    or their loved ones.

God redeems our life from the Pit:
From the depths of despair.
He crowns us with mercy and love:
Here and in all eternity.

O Lord, open our lips:
To praise you the God of love.
In this is love, not that we loved God:
But that he loves us forever.

READING: MARK 12:28-33

Jesus Pronounces the Great Commandment

A teacher of the Law was there who heard the discussion. He saw that Jesus had given the Sadducees a good answer, so he came to him with a question: 'Which commandment is the most important of all?'

Jesus replied, 'The most important one is this: "Listen, Israel! The Lord our God is the only Lord. Love the Lord your God with all your heart, with all your soul, with all your mind, and with all your strength." The second most important commandment is this: "Love your neighbour as you love yourself." There is no other commandment more important than these two.'

The teacher of the Law said to Jesus, 'Well done, Teacher! It is true, as you say, that only the Lord is God and that there is no other god but he. And man must love God with all his heart and with all his mind and with all his strength; and he must love his neighbour as he loves himself. It is more important to obey these two commandments than to offer animals and other sacrifices to God.'

READING: LINES BY HORATIO BONAR, BASED ON 1 JOHN 4:7-8

Beloved, let us love:
  For love is light,
And he who loveth not
  Dwelleth in night.

Beloved, let us love:
  for only thus

Shall we behold that God
  Who loveth us.

PICTURE • PONDER • PRAY • PROMISE

A PRAYER

  Glorious and wonderful are you, our God,
  For we see your beauty in each act of love:
  Make our minds clear to discern
  How love explains your truth and makes you known.
    Amen.

Thank God that he loves us all.

Thank God for sins and silliness forgiven.

Pray for those who seem to have no-one to love them,
  that they may find God's love from others.

  The law of the Lord is perfect:
  Reviving the soul.
  The commands of the Lord are true:
  They make the simple wise.
  Let us love:
  For love is from God.

O Lord, open our lips:
To praise your commandments and power.
Your wisdom will live for ever:
Your grace is sufficient for us.

READING: MARK 12:37B-44

Jesus Defines True Devotion

A large crowd was listening to Jesus gladly. As he taught them, he said, 'Watch out for the teachers of the Law, who like to walk around in their long robes and be greeted with respect in the market-place, who choose the reserved seats in the synagogues and the best places at feasts. They take advantage of widows and rob them of their homes, and then make a show of saying long prayers. Their punishment will be all the worse!'

As Jesus sat near the temple treasury, he watched the people as they dropped in their money. Many rich men dropped in a lot of money; then a poor widow came along and dropped in two little copper coins, worth about a penny. He called his disciples together and said to them, 'I tell you that this poor widow put more in the offering box than all the others. For the others put in what they had to spare of their riches; but she, poor as she is, put in all she had – she gave all she had to live on.'

READING: LINES FROM ISAIAH 29: 13-14 (RSV)

And the Lord said:
Because this people draw near with their mouth
And honour me with their lips,
While their hearts are far from me,
And their fear of me is a commandment of men
Learned by rote;
I will do marvellous things with these people,
Wonderful and marvellous;
And the wisdom of their wise men shall perish,
And the discernment of discerners shall be hid.

PICTURE · PONDER · PRAY · PROMISE

A PRAYER

> Holy Spirit, Wisdom and Love,
> Make us wise with true insight,
> Fill us with true devotion. Amen.

Thank God that Jesus has revealed his true nature.

Thank God for those holy people whom you know.

Pray for those who are besotted by wealth and power.

Pray to be Jesus-centred in mind and deed.

> The Lord sees the truth about all mankind:
> **The false and the proud he abhors.**
> Keep our hearts pure, O Lord:
> **Pure and entirely for you.**

O Lord, open our lips:
To praise you in faith and trust.
The world has its troubles and pain:
But you are its healer and king.

READING: LINES BY MARTIN LUTHER

A safe stronghold our God is still,
A trusty shield and weapon;
He'll keep us clear from all the ill
That hath us now o'ertaken.
The ancient prince of hell
Hath risen with purpose fell;
Strong mail of craft and power
He weareth in this hour;
On earth is not his fellow.

With force of arms we nothing can,
Full soon were we down-ridden;
But for us fights the proper Man,
Whom God himself hath bidden.
Ask ye, Who is this same?
Christ Jesus is his name,
The Lord Sabaoth's Son;
He, and no other one,
Shall conquer in the battle.

READING: MARK 13:1-8

Jesus Speaks of the World's Evils

As Jesus was leaving the Temple, one of his disciples said, 'Look, Teacher! What wonderful stones and buildings!'

Jesus answered, 'You see these great buildings? Not a single stone here will be left in its place; every one of them will be thrown down.'

Jesus was sitting on the Mount of Olives, across from the Temple, when Peter, James, John and Andrew came to him in private. 'Tell us when this will be,' they said, 'and tell us what will happen to show that the time has come for all these thing to take place.'

Jesus said to them, 'Be on guard, and don't let anyone deceive you. Many men, claiming to speak for me, will come and say, 'I am he!' and they will deceive many people. And don't be troubled when you hear the noise of battles close by and news of battles far away. Such things must happen, but they do not mean that the end has come. Countries will fight each other; kingdoms will attack one another. There will be earthquakes everywhere, and there will be famines. These things are like the first pains of childbirth.

PICTURE · PONDER · PRAY · PROMISE

A PRAYER

> Keep us faithful, Lord,
> Faithful when we are scared,
> Faithful when we are bored,
> Faithful when we are tired,
> Faithful amid all busy-ness.
> For you alone are our true Lord. Amen.

Thank God for faith in a world of evil.

Pray for peace between
> nations
> races
> individual people.

Pray for peace and compassion in the hearts of those who have power in society.

Pray for the strength to keep faith with God.

> In the world there is tribulation:
> **But Christ has conquered the world.**
> Lord, may we keep faith with you:
> **As you are faithful to us.**

O Lord, open our lips:
To praise you the strength in our lives.
You are a tower of strength:
To all who revere your name.

READING: MARK 13:9-13

Jesus Tells of Persecution

'You yourselves must be on guard. You will be arrested and taken to court. You will be beaten in the synagogues; you will stand before rulers and kings for my sake to tell them the Good News. But before the end comes, the gospel must be preached to all peoples. And when you are arrested and taken to court, do not worry beforehand about what you are going to say; when the time comes, say whatever is then given to you. For the words you speak will not be yours; they will come from the Holy Spirit. Men will hand over their own brothers to be put to death, and fathers will do the same to their children. Children will turn against their parents and have them put to death. Everyone will hate you because of me. But whoever holds out to the end will be saved.'

READING: PSALM 41:1,7-11

Blessed is he that considers the poor and helpless:
    The Lord will deliver him in the day of trouble.
All those that hate me whisper together against me:
    They devise plots against me.
They say, 'A deadly thing has got hold of him:
    He will not get up again from where he lies.'
Even my bosom friend in whom I trusted:
    Who shared my bread; has lifted his heel against me.
But you O Lord be gracious and raise me up:
    And I will repay them what they have deserved.
By this I will know that you favour me:
    That my enemy shall not triumph over me.

PICTURE · PONDER · PRAY · PROMISE

A PRAYER

> Bless and heal, O Lord,
> All who betray and are cruel:
> Bless and heal, O Lord,
> All victims of violence and hate.
> Bless and heal your world,
> So broken by malice and greed. Amen.

Praise God for the martyrs of the Christian faith.

Pray for those who suffer because of the fear and hatred of others.

Pray for yourself and all Christian people
> for strength and power to keep faith
> under persecution in word or in actions.

> In you, O Lord, we put our trust:
> **We declare, 'You are our God'.**
> Let us be strong in faith:
> **Your grace is sufficient for us.**

As watchmen wait for the morning:
We long for you, O God.
O Lord, open our lips:
Make us joyful to speak in your praise.

READING: PSALM 63:1-5

O God you are my God:
    eagerly will I seek you.
My soul thirsts for you, my flesh longs for you:
    as a dry and thirsty land where no water is.
So it was when I beheld you in the sanctuary:
    and saw your power and your glory.
For your unchanging goodness is better than life:
    therefore my lips shall praise you.
And so I will bless you as long as I live:
    and in your name will I lift my hands on high.

READING: MARK 13:28-37

Christian Watchfulness

'Let the fig-tree teach you a lesson. When its branches become green and tender and it starts putting out leaves, you know that summer is near. In the same way, when you see these things happening, you will know that the time is near, ready to begin. Remember that all these things will happen before the people now living have all died. Heaven and earth will pass away, but my words will never pass away.

'No-one knows, however, when that day or hour will come – neither the angels in heaven, nor the Son; only the Father knows. Be on watch, be alert, for you do not know when the time will come. It will be like a man who goes away from home on a journey and leaves his servants in charge, after giving to each one his own work to do and after telling the doorkeeper to keep watch. Be on guard, then, because you do not know

when the master of the house is coming – it might be in
the evening or at midnight or before dawn or at sunrise.
If he comes suddenly, he must not find you asleep. What
I say to you, then, I say to all: Watch!'

PICTURE • PONDER • PRAY • PROMISE

A Prayer

Lord of life, God of Eternity,
Master of History, Ruler of all creation.
We praise you for ever.
Make us alert to you,
Ready to hear your voice
For you alone are truly wise.

Praise God for Jesus whose life reveals truth
and exposes falsehood.

Pray to be alert to the meaning of our faith
in daily living.

Pray for those who think they have no need of God.

Pray for those who have false gods, such as money,
drugs or fame.

Praise God that He is King who will draw creation
into his loving power at the end of time.

Lord, your word is forever:
It stand firm in the heavens.
You are the Lord of eternity:
And the Master of time.

O Lord, open our lips:
And our mouth shall proclaim your praise.
Let the love in our prayers be a perfume:
To fill all our days with your love.

READING: MARK 14:1-9

Jesus is Anointed

It was now two days before the Festival of Passover and Unleavened Bread. The chief priests and teachers of the Law were looking for a way to arrest Jesus secretly and put him to death. 'We must not do it during the festival,' they said, 'or the people might riot.'

Jesus was in Bethany at the house of Simon, a man who had suffered from a dreaded skin-disease. While Jesus was eating, a woman came in with an alabaster jar full of a very expensive perfume made of pure nard. She broke the jar and poured the perfume on Jesus' head. Some of the people there became angry and said to one another, 'What was the use of wasting the perfume? It could have been sold for more than three hundred silver coins and the money given to the poor!' And they criticised her harshly.

But Jesus said, 'Leave her alone! Why are you bothering her? She has done a fine and beautiful thing for me. You will always have poor people with you, and any time you want to, you can help them. But you will not always have me. She did what she could; she poured perfume on my body to prepare it ahead of time for burial. Now, I assure you that wherever the gospel is preached all over the world, what she has done will be told in memory of her.'

READING: LINES BY J. S. B. MONSELL

O worship the Lord in the beauty of holiness!
Bow down before him, his glory proclaim;
With gold of obedience and incense of lowliness,
Kneel and adore him: the Lord is his name.

Low at his feet lay thy burden of carefulness.
High on his heart he will bear it for thee,
Comfort thy sorrows, and answer thy prayerfulness,
Guiding thy steps as may best for thee be.

PICTURE · PONDER · PRAY · PROMISE

A PRAYER

Jesus, Lord and friend,
may the love you have for us
inspire us to show your love to others
so that they may know you too. Amen.

Thank God for love received and given.

Thank him that we can love him through other people.

Pray for the ability to care.

Pray for those whom society despises.

If we do not love those whom we have seen:
How can we love God whom we have not seen?
We love him now:
Because he first loved us.

O Lord, open our lips:
To praise you in fellowship and faith.
You have given the Eucharist:
To make us one in you.

READING: MARK 14:12-25

Jesus at the Last Supper

On the first day of the Festival of Unleavened Bread, the day the lambs for the Passover meal were killed, Jesus' disciples asked him, 'Where do you want us to go and get the Passover meal ready for you?'

Then Jesus sent two of them with these instructions: 'Go into the city, and a man carrying a jar of water will meet you. Follow him to the house he enters, and say to the owner of the house 'The Teacher says, "Where is the room where my disciples and I will eat the Passover meal?" Then he will show you a large upstairs room, prepared and furnished, where you will get everything ready for us.'

The disciples left, went to the city, and found everything just as Jesus had told them; and they prepared the Passover meal.

When it was evening, Jesus came with the twelve disciples. While they were at the table eating, Jesus said, 'I tell you that one of you will betray me - one who is eating with me.'

The disciples were upset and began to ask him, one after the other, 'Surely you don't mean me, do you?'

Jesus answered, 'It will be one of you twelve, one who dips his bread in the dish with me. The Son of Man will die as the Scriptures say he will; but how terrible for that man who betrays the Son of Man! It would have been better for that man if he had never been born!'

While they were eating, Jesus took a piece of bread, gave a prayer of thanks, broke it, and gave it to his disciples. 'Take it,' he said, 'this is my body.'

Then he took a cup, gave thanks to God, and handed it to them; and they all drank from it. Jesus said, 'This is my blood which is poured out for many, my blood which seals God's covenant. I tell you, I will never again drink this wine until the day I drink the new wine in the Kingdom of God.'

READING: LINES OF THOMAS AQUINAS

At the last great supper lying
Circled by his brethren's band,
Jesus, with the law complying,
First he finished its command,
Then, immortal Food supplying,
Gave himself with his own hand.

Word made Flesh, by word he maketh
Very bread his Flesh to be;
Man in wine Christ's Blood partaketh:
And if senses fail to see,
Faith alone, the true heart waketh
To behold the mystery.

PICTURE · PONDER · PRAY · PROMISE

A PRAYER

O God, in this wonderful sacrament,
You have given us the memorial of
    the passion of your Son, Jesus Christ.
Grant us so to reverence these sacred
    mysteries of his body and blood,
That we may know in ourselves the fruits
    of the Holy Spirit. Amen.

Thank God for the Holy Communion.

Pray to learn more of its meaning and its grace.

Pray for the unity of all Christian people.

Pray that the Communion will help us to follow the
Way of the Cross.

> As often as we eat the bread and share the cup:
> **We proclaim our Lord's death and resurrection.**
> May we be dead to sin:
> **And alive to right living in Christ.**

O Lord, open our lips:
To rejoice in the strength of your mercy.
Our help comes only from the Lord:
Who has made heaven and earth.

READING: MARK 14:26-31, 66-72

Jesus Predicts Peter's Denial

Then they sang a hymn and went out to the Mount of Olives. Jesus said to them, 'All of you will run away and leave me, for the scripture says, "God will kill the shepherd, and the sheep will be scattered." But after I am raised to life, I will go to Galilee ahead of you.'

Peter answered, 'I will never leave you, even though all the rest do!'

Jesus said to Peter, 'I tell you that before the cock crows twice tonight, you will say three times that you do not know me.'

Peter answered even more strongly, 'I will never say that, even if I have to die with you!'

And all the other disciples said the same thing.

Peter's Denial

Peter was still down in the courtyard when one of the High Priest's servant-girls came by. When she saw Peter warming himself, she looked straight at him and said, 'You, too, were with Jesus of Nazareth.'

But he denied it. 'I don't know . . . I don't understand what you are talking about,' he answered, and went out into the passage. Just then a cock crowed.

The servant-girl saw him there and began to repeat to the bystanders, 'He is one of them!' But Peter denied it again.

A little while later the bystanders accused Peter again, 'You can't deny that you are one of them, because you, too, are from Galilee.'

Then Peter said, 'I swear that I am telling the truth! May God punish me if I am not! I do not know the man you are talking about!'

Just then a cock crowed a second time, and Peter remembered how Jesus had said to him, 'Before the cock crows twice, you will say three times that you do not know me.' And he broke down and cried.

READING: 'PETER'

'You are the Christ!' Peter exclaimed,
And proud he was to be the first
To know the truth and have it named.
'I'll never leave you Christ!'

And, then, alarm! A spiteful crowd
Came on, and with the rest he fled.
He warmed himself, no longer proud
And wished that he were dead.

Christ, still today your searching face
Cuts through corruption, lies and fears
To shine a light in every place
On Peters down the years.

PICTURE · PONDER · PRAY · PROMISE

A PRAYER

Father of all mankind,
You know us as we really are,
And yet still love us.
Grant that from the example of
    Simon Peter
We may learn to receive your mercy
    and forgiveness. Amen.

Praise God for his generous mercy.

Praise him that he releases us from guilt and sin

Pray to grow more able to forgive and be forgiven.

Pray for people who cannot or dare not forgive others.

The greatness of God's mercy:
Fills the creation.
The power of his mercy:
Sets us free.

O Lord, open our lips:
To be with you in mind and spirit.
Help us to watch and pray:
As you suffer for us.

READING: MARK 14:32-52

Jesus in Distress

They came to a place called Gethsemane, and Jesus said to his disciples, 'Sit here while I pray.' He took Peter, James and John with him. Distress and anguish came over him, and he said to them, 'The sorrow in my heart is so great that it almost crushes me. Stay here and keep watch.'

He went a little farther on, threw himself on the ground, and prayed that, if possible, he might not have to go through that time of suffering. 'Father,' he prayed, 'my Father! All things are possible for you. Take this cup of suffering away from me. Yet not what I want, but what you want.'

Then he returned and found the three disciples asleep. He said to Peter, 'Simon, are you asleep? Weren't you able to stay awake even for one hour?' And he said to them, 'Keep watch, and pray that you will not fall into temptation. The spirit is willing but the flesh is weak.'

He went away once more and prayed, saying the same words. Then he came back to the disciples and found them asleep; they could not keep their eyes open. And they did not know what to say to him.

When he came back the third time, he said to them, 'Are you still sleeping and resting? Enough! The hour has come! Look, the Son of Man is now being handed over to the power of sinful men. Get up, let us go. Look, here is the man who is betraying me!'

Jesus was still speaking when Judas, one of the twelve disciples, arrived. With him was a crowd armed with swords and clubs, and sent by the chief priests, the teachers of the Law, and the elders. The traitor had given the crowd a signal: 'The man I kiss is the one you want. Arrest him and take him away under guard.'

As soon as Judas arrived, he went up to Jesus and said, 'Teacher!' and kissed him. So they arrested Jesus and held him tight. But one of those standing there drew his sword and struck at the High Priest's slave, cutting off his ear. Then Jesus spoke up and said to them, 'Did you have to come with swords and clubs to capture me, as though I were an outlaw? Day after day I was with you teaching in the Temple, and you did not arrest me. But the Scriptures must come true.'

Then all the disciples left him and ran away.

A certain young man, dressed only in a linen-cloth, was following Jesus. They tried to arrest him, but he ran away naked, leaving the cloth behind.

READING: PSALM 62:1-5

My soul waits in silence for God:
    for from him comes my salvation.
He only is my rock and my salvation:
    my strong tower so that I shall never be moved.
How long will you plot against a man to destroy him:
    as though he were a leaning fence or a buckling wall?
Their design is to thrust him from his height
    and their delight is in lies:
They bless with their lips but inwardly they curse.
Nevertheless, my soul, wait in silence for God:
    for from him comes my hope.

PICTURE • PONDER • PRAY • PROMISE

A Prayer

> We confess, O Lord, the sins which fill you with sorrow,
> and the apathy with which we treat your love.
> Forgive us, keep us true to you
> in all our days. Amen.

Thank God for Jesus who bore alone the pain and evil of the world.

Pray for all those who are under stress and sorrow.

Pray for those tempted to betray others.

Pray forgivingly for anyone who has betrayed you.

> God bought mankind:
> **with his heart's blood expense.**
> A man sold God:
> **for thirty silver pence.**
> Yet Christ did win the victory of love.

The final response is based partly on words by Robert Herrick

O Lord, open our lips:
To praise your suffering death
You were despised and rejected:
Yet in dying you saved the world.

READING: MARK 14: 53-65

Jesus Accused

Then Jesus was taken to the High priest's house, where all the chief priests, the elders, and the teachers of the Law were gathering. Peter followed from a distance and went into the courtyard of the High Priest's house. There he sat down with the guards, keeping himself warm by the fire. The chief priests and the whole Council tried to find some evidence against Jesus in order to put him to death, but they could not find any. Many witnesses told lies against Jesus, but their stories did not agree.

Then some men stood up and told this lie against Jesus: 'We heard him say, "I will tear down this Temple which men have made, and after three days I will build one that is not made by men."'

Not even they, however, could make their stories agree.

The High Priest stood up in front of them all and questioned Jesus, 'Have you no answer to the accusation they bring against you?'

But Jesus kept quiet and would not say a word. Again the High Priest questioned him, 'Are you the Messiah, the Son of the Blessed God?'

'I am,' answered Jesus, 'and you will all see the Son of Man seated on the right of the Almighty and coming with the clouds of heaven!'

The High Priest tore his robes and said, 'We don't need any more witnesses! You heard his blasphemy. What is your decision?'

They all voted against him: he was guilty and should be put to death.

Some of them began to spit on Jesus, and they blindfolded him and hit him. 'Guess who hit you!' they said. And the guards took him and slapped him.

READING: LINES BY WILLIAM BLAKE

Cruelty has a Human Heart,
And Jealousy a Human Face;
Terror the Human Form Divine,
And Secrecy the Human Dress.

The Human Dress is forged Iron,
The Human Form a fiery Forge,
The Human Face a Furnace sealed,
The Human heart its hungry Gorge.

PICTURE • PONDER • PRAY • PROMISE

A PRAYER

Jesus, Lord and Saviour:
As you were rejected by those you came to serve,
May we learn never to reject the truth,
Never to despise those whom we meet,
and never fail to show your love to others:
Lord, give us hearts open to love! Amen.

Praise God that He was ready to suffer for our sake.

Praise God for the martyrs who have suffered for Christ's sake.

Pray for the persecuted, the neglected and starving people of the world.

Pray for strength to put Christ first in all things.

He was despised and rejected by mankind:
A man of sorrows and acquainted with grief.
He was wounded because of our sins:
He was bruised because of our evil.
He died as a criminal:
He lives as Lord of eternal life.

O Lord, open our lips:
To adore you, crucified for us.
You were despised and rejected:
Yet in dying you saved the world.

READING: LINES BY ISAAC WATTS

When I survey the wondrous Cross
On which the Prince of Glory died,
My richest gain I count but loss,
And pour contempt on all my pride.

Forbid it, Lord, that I should boast
Save in the Cross of Christ my God;
All the vain things that charm me most,
I sacrifice them to his Blood.

See from his head, his hands, his feet,
Sorrow and love flow mingled down;
Did e'er such love and sorrow meet,
Or thorns compose so rich a crown?

Were the whole realm of nature mine,
That were an offering far too small;
Love so amazing, so divine,
Demands my soul, my life, my all.

READING: MARK 15:1-39

Jesus is Crucified

Early in the morning the chief priests met hurriedly with the elders, the teachers of the Law, and the whole Council, and made their plans. They put Jesus in chains, led him away, and handed him over to Pilate. Pilate questioned him, 'Are you the king of the Jews?'

Jesus answered, 'So you say.'

The chief priests were accusing Jesus of many things, so Pilate questioned him again, 'Aren't you going to answer? Listen to all their accusations!'

Again Jesus refused to say a word, and Pilate was amazed.

At every Passover Festival Pilate was in the habit of setting free any one prisoner asked for. At that time a man named Barabbas was in prison with the rebels who had committed murder in the riot. When the crowd gathered and began to ask Pilate for the usual favour, he asked them, 'Do you want me to set free for you the king of the Jews?' He knew very well that the chief priests had handed Jesus over to him because they were jealous.

But the chief priests stirred up the crowd to ask, instead, for Pilate to set Barabbas free for them. Pilate spoke again to the crowd, 'What, then, do you want me to do with the one you call the king of the Jews?'

They shouted back, 'Crucify him!'

'But what crime has he committed?' Pilate asked.

They shouted all the louder, 'Crucify him!'

Pilate wanted to please the crowd, so he set Barabbas free for them. Then he had Jesus whipped and handed him over to be crucified.

The soldiers took Jesus inside to the courtyard of the governor's palace and called together the rest of the company. They put a purple robe on Jesus, made a crown out of thorny branches, and put it on his head. Then they began to salute him: 'Long live the King of the Jews!' They beat him over the head with a stick, spat on him, fell on their knees and bowed down to him. When they had finished mocking him, they took off the purple robe and put his own clothes back on him. Then they led him out to crucify him.

On the way they met a man named Simon, who was coming into the city from the country, and the soldiers forced him to carry Jesus' cross. (Simon was from Cyrene and was the father of Alexander and Rufus.) They took Jesus to a place called Golgotha, which means 'The Place of the Skull'. There they tried to give him wine mixed with a drug called myrrh, but Jesus would not drink it. Then they crucified him and divided his clothes among themselves, throwing dice to see who would get which piece of clothing. It was nine o'clock in the morning when they crucified him. The notice of the accusation against him said: 'The King of the Jews'. They also crucified two bandits with Jesus, one on his right and the other on his left.*

People passing by shook their heads and hurled insults at Jesus: 'Aha! You were going to tear down the Temple and build it up again in three days! Now come down from the cross and save yourself!'

In the same way the chief priests and the teachers of the Law jeered at Jesus, saying to each other, 'He saved others, but he cannot save himself! Let us see the Messiah, the king of Israel come down from the cross now, and we will believe in him!'

And the two who were crucified with Jesus insulted him also.

At noon the whole country was covered with darkness, which lasted for three hours. At three o'clock Jesus cried out with a loud shout, 'Eloi, Eloi, lema sabachthani?' which means, 'My God my God, why did you abandon me?'

Some of the people there heard him and said, 'Listen, he is calling for Elijah!' One of them ran up with a sponge, soaked it in cheap wine, and put it on the end of a stick. Then he held it up to Jesus' lips and said, 'Wait! Let us see if Elijah is coming to bring him down from the cross!' With a loud cry Jesus died.

The curtain hanging in the Temple was torn in two, from top to bottom. The army officer who was standing there in front of the cross saw how Jesus had died. 'This man was really the Son of God!' he said.

* Some manuscripts add here: In this way the scripture came true which says, 'He shared the fate of criminals.'

PICTURE · PONDER · PRAY · PROMISE

A PRAYER

> Lord, you have given your all for mankind:
> Help us to give our all to you. Amen.

Praise Christ who has died to save us all.

Praise Christ who has conquered sin and death.

Pray to feel deeply the suffering of Jesus.

Pray to feel deeply the love which made him suffer.

> Truly, this man was the Son of God!
> **Our Lord for ever and ever.**
> He died because of our sins:
> **To break evil and death for ever.**
> Love so amazing, so divine:
> **Demands our soul, our life, our all.**

O Lord, open our lips:
To adore you at rest in the tomb.
We wait in the heaviness of grief:
In the hope of your glory.

READING: LINES FROM THE 'STABAT MATER'

At the Cross her vigil keeping,
Stood the mourning Mother weeping,
Close to Jesus at the last.
Through her soul, with sadness aching,
Bowed with anguish, deeply grieving,
Now the painful sword has passed.

Who on Christ's dear Mother gazing,
In her trouble so amazing,
Born of woman, would not weep?
Who on his dear Mother thinking,
Such a cup of sorrow drinking,
Would not share her sorrow deep?

READING: MARK 15:40-47

Jesus is Laid in the Tomb

Some women were there, looking on from a distance. Among them were Mary Magdalene, Mary the mother of the younger James and of Joseph, and Salome. They had followed Jesus while he was in Galilee and had helped him. Many other women who had come to Jerusalem with him were there also.

It was towards evening when Joseph of Arimathea arrived. He was a respected member of the Council, who was waiting for the coming of the Kingdom of God. It was Preparation day (that is, the day before the Sabbath), so Joseph went boldly into the presence of Pilate and asked him for the body of Jesus. Pilate was surprised to hear that Jesus was already dead. He called the army officer and asked him if Jesus had been dead a long time. After hearing the officer's report, Pilate told Joseph he could have the body. Joseph bought a linen sheet, took the body down, wrapped it in the sheet, and placed it in a tomb which had been dug out of solid rock. Then he rolled a large stone across the entrance to the tomb. Mary Magdalene and Mary the mother of Joseph were watching and saw where the body of Jesus was placed.

PICTURE · PONDER · PRAY · PROMISE

A PRAYER

> Lord, we praise you for Mary and her courageous
>   love for Jesus.
> May her example be our inspiration to follow
>   you with all our heart. Amen.

Thank God for our mothers.

Thank God for Christ's steadfast love.

Pray for faith to hold fast in the bad times
   as well as the good.

Pray for those who grieve for loved ones,
   especially those who grieve without hope.

> Jesus said: 'Destroy this temple:
> **And in three days I will raise it up'**
> He spoke:
> **Of the temple of his body.**
> Heaviness may endure for a night:
> **But joy comes with the morning.**

Christ is risen!
He is risen indeed!
Death is defeated!
Sin is overcome!
O Lord, open our lips:
To praise you with all our heart.

READING: MARK 16:1-8

Resurrection: Joy, Amazement and Fear

After the Sabbath was over, Mary Magdalene, Mary the mother of James, and Salome bought spices to go and anoint the body of Jesus. Very early on Sunday morning, at sunrise, they went to the tomb. On the way they said to one another, 'Who will roll away the stone for us from the entrance to the tomb?' (It was a very large stone). Then they looked up and saw that the stone had already been rolled back. So they entered the tomb, where they saw a young man sitting on the right, wearing a white robe – and they were alarmed.

'Don't be alarmed,' he said. 'I know you are looking for Jesus of Nazareth, who was crucified. He is not here – he has been raised! Look, here is the place where they put him. Now go and give this message to his disciples, including Peter: "He is going to Galilee ahead of you; there you will see him, just as he told you."'

So they went out and ran from the tomb, distressed and terrified. They said nothing to anyone, because they were afraid.

READING: LINES BY HENRY VAUGHAN

Resurrection: Joy Realised

Death and darkness, get you packing,
Nothing now to man is lacking,
All your triumphs now are ended,
And what Adam marred, is mended.

PICTURE • PONDER • PRAY • PROMISE

Almighty Father,
We praise and adore you for the
   Resurrection of Jesus:

Almighty Jesus,
We rejoice with you at your conquest
   of sin and death:

Almighty Spirit,
We rejoice with you at the coming
   of new life from the grave:

Grant us to live the resurrection life,
here and in heaven. Amen.

Jesus Lord,

We thank you for the gift of Lent
  and for the crowning happiness of Easter.

May we always grow
   to know you more clearly
   love you more dearly
   follow you more nearly,
   day by day. Amen.

They ran from the resurrection tomb:
In sorrow and amazement.
Christ came to meet them:
And the sorrow was turned to joy!